BEAR HUGS

FOR

_____

FROM

_____

Your love has given me great
joy and encouragement.

Philemon 7

BEAR HUGS FOR MOMS

Copyright 2002 by Zondervan
ISBN 0-310-98834-9

Requests for information should be addressed to:

Inspirio, The gift group of Zondervan
Grand Rapids, Michigan 49530
http://www.inspiriogifts.com

Compiler and writer: Doris Rikkers
Associate Editor: Molly Detweiler
Project Manager: Patti Matthews
Design: Mark Veldheer
Photography: Photographic Concepts

Printed in China
02 03 04/HK/4 3 2 1

BEAR HUGS

FOR MOMS

inspirio

My Mom

is sweeter than honey!

Thank you, Mom,
for all your love
For teaching me
about God above
For helping me to
learn and grow
For all these things
I love you so!

There's nothing better
when you're sick than
Mom's tender care!

Hugs are the flowers of a mother's love.

D. Wynn

The cheerful voice, the happy laughter of a mother, make home a lovely place to be.

Elizabeth Beck

A mother who loves her
children imitates God's
love for us, His children.

Christopher de Vinck

God is love.
Whoever lives in love lives in God, and God in him.

I John 4:16

The happiness of life
is made up of
minute fractions—
a kiss or smile,
a kind look, a heart–
felt compliment.

William Scott

I am beary
thankful
for you!
I love you
beary much!

Who ran to help me when I fell,
And would some pretty story tell,
Or kiss the place to make it well?
My mother.

Ann Taylor

A mother

understands what a
child does not say.

A cheerful look brings
joy to the heart.

Proverbs 15:30

Mom, thanks for being
my cheerleader.

Blowing bubbles knows no age.
Young and old forget their days.
Happy thoughts and
joy-filled giggles
Join our hearts together.

E. Beck

Sweet sleep starts
with a mother's hug
and a goodnight kiss.

D. Rikkers

Who takes the child by the hand
Takes the mother by the heart.

Danish proverb

A godly
mother raises
her child in
righteousness
and love.

D. Wynn

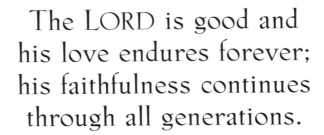

The LORD is good and
his love endures forever;
his faithfulness continues
through all generations.

Psalm 100:5

In raising children,
all you can do
is your best...
we take care of the
possible and leave the
impossible to God.

Ruth Bell Graham

Fear is unknown in a
mother's loving arms.

E. Beck

There is no fear in love.
Perfect love drives out fear.

1 John 4:18

Taste and see

that the LORD *is* good.

Psalm 34:8

A mother's love is like a
homemade pie, it warms
me inside and out, in both
my heart and my tummy!

If I had more than one heart to give,
I'd give them all to my Mom.

D. Wynn

M is for the mercy she possesses,
O means that I owe her all I own.
T is for her tender sweet caresses,
H is for her hands that made a home;
E means everything she's done to
 help me
R means Real and Regular, you see,

Put them all together they spell
"Mother"
A word that means the world to me!

Howard Johnson

The LORD bless you and keep you;
the LORD make his face shine
upon you and be gracious to you;
the LORD turn his face toward
you and give you peace.

Numbers 6:24–26

Mom:

You make our home a happy one.
You make my life so sweet.
You give me hugs and kisses
that make my world complete.

D. Rikkers

Mother, you
always know when
to hold on tight…
and when to let go
of my hand so I can
walk on my own.

D. Wynn

A mother's love is a glimpse of heaven.

E. Beck

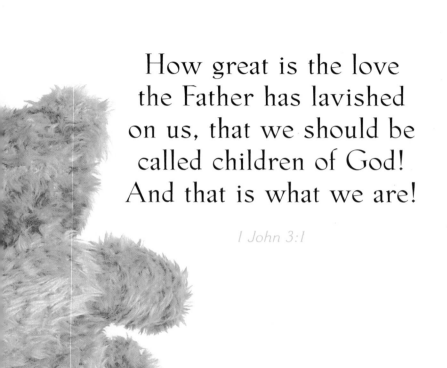

How great is the love
the Father has lavished
on us, that we should be
called children of God!
And that is what we are!

I John 3:1

I send you, Mom, this message,
a message filled with love
Because I know that you're a gift,
sent straight from God above!

Motherhood is a partnership with God.

A mother's love is like God's love; He loves us not because we are lovable, but because it is His nature to love, and because we are His children.

Earl Riney

You can never duck a
mother's love. It's with you
no matter where you go.

D. Wynn

Mom, thanks for always encouraging me to make lemonade when life gives me lemons!

You make
me glad by
your deeds,
O LORD;
I sing for
joy at the
works of
your hands.

Psalm 92:4

My heart bubbles over
with love for you.

Mom's recipe to make
everything right:
A warm bath.
A little nap.
And a cup of hot cocoa.

Arlene Keeling

Your love makes me want to celebrate with joy!

Like a handmade sweater,
warm and cozy is your love,
No matter what the size,
your love fits me like a glove.

Thank you, Mom, for loving me so much that you taught me how to spread love to others.

Youth fades;
love droops;
the leaves of
friendship fall;
A mother's
secret hope
outlives them all.

Oliver Wendell Holmes

A godly mother mirrors God's love. Thank you for reflecting God's love into my life.

D. Rikkers

Mercy, peace and love be yours in abundance.

Jude 2

I love you, Mom!

SOURCES:

de Vinck, Christopher. *The Book of Moonlight*. Grand Rapids, MI: Zondervan, 1998. Simple Wonders. Grand Rapids, MI: Zondervan, 1995.

God's Little Devotional Book for Moms. Tulsa, OK: Honor Books, Inc., 1995.

Women's Devotional Bible. Grand Rapids, MI: Zondervan, 1990.

The Women's Study Bible. Nashville, TN: Thomas Nelson Publishers, 1995.